Presented to _____

on_____
 (date)

"Thank you, teacher, for

_____

_____

_____ "

The Best Thing About My Teacher

The Best Thing About My Teacher

Notes of appreciation from students

By Judy Gordon Morrow

BROADMAN
&HOLMAN
PUBLISHERS

Nashville, Tennessee

© 1999 by Judy Gordon Morrow
All rights reserved
Printed in the United States of America

0-8054-1661-7

Published by Broadman & Holman Publishers, Nashville, Tennessee
Editorial Team: Vicki Crumpton, Janis Whipple, Kim Overcash
Page Design: Paul T. Gant Art & Design
Typesetting: PerfecType, Nashville, Tennessee

Dewey Decimal Classification: 371.102
Subject Heading: TEACHER-STUDENT RELATIONSHIPS / TEACHERS—QUOTATIONS
Library of Congress Card Catalog Number: 98-37670

Library of Congress Cataloging-in-Publication Data

Morrow, Judy Gordon
    The best thing about my teacher : notes of appreciation from students / [compiled and
    edited by] Judy Gordon Morrow.
       p. cm.
    ISBN 0-8054-1661-7 (pbk.)
1. Teacher-student relationships—Miscellaneous. 2. Teachers—Quotations. 3. Students—
Quotations.
I. Morrow, Judy Gordon.
LB1033.B487   1999
371.102'3—dc21

                  98-37670
                  CIP

2 3 4 5 03 02 01 00 99

Dedication

With gratitude to all dedicated teachers,

and with special thanks to

Janet Holm McHenry,

teacher, writer, and friend extraordinaire.

Acknowledgments

Thank you to the following teachers and parents who helped gather the children's responses:

Virginia Ball
Pat Boyer
Ruth Carnell
Yvonne Casalnuovo
Jason Clark
Becky Cobb
Pat Crosby
Madeline D'Andrea
Bob Dickinson
Darla Draper

Brenda Farley
Nancy Gordon
Tricia Goyer
Michele Graham
Andrea Grinnell
Sue Gutierrez
Susan Hagwood
Julie Hochrein
Joy Jackson
Susan Jackson

Cathy Jones
Jan Kern
Pauline Kimmel
Holly La Chappel
Kathy Manus
Cindy Martinusen
Janet Holm McHenry
Annette McTighe
Shelly Morrow
Vicki Murray
Christine Peters
Loretta Ramirez
Michael Rodriguez
JoAnne Rotta

Susan Salucci
Betsy Schaffer
Ellen Schwartz
Diane Seibel
Don Shaw
Nancy Sipe
Adrienne Stenson
Pamela Townsend
Joan Turner
Susanne Vaughn
Mary Vossler
Donna Weber
Jeanne Williams

The Best Thing About My Teacher...

ABCDEFGHIJKLMNOPQRSTUVWXYZ
abcdefghijklmnopqrstuvwxyz 1234567890

The best thing about my teacher is she hugs.
(Age 6)

The best thing about my teacher is she is never
snappy and mean. (Age 16)

The best thing about my teacher is
she's nice, yet strict. (Age 11)

ABCDEFGHIJKLMNOPQRSTUVWXYZ
abcdefghijklmnopqrstuvwxyz 1234567890

The best thing about my teacher is letting us go up in front of the class to share something. (Age 7)

The best thing about my teacher is her overall personality—she's bright and witty, with much to offer. (Age 17)

The best thing about my teacher is when she says, "Oh, Johnny is absent. I will miss him." (Age 5)

3

ABCDEFGHIJKLMNOPQRSTUVWXYZ
abcdefghijklmnopqrstuvwxyz 1234567890

The best thing about my teacher is she will never let a kid fall behind. (Age 11)

The best thing about my teacher is he really cares about me. (Age 8)

The best thing about my teacher is her ability to teach and care about her students as if they were her own, and not having any favorites. (Age 17)

4

ABCDEFGHIJKLMNOPQRSTUVWXYZ
abcdefghijklmnopqrstuvwxyz 1234567890

The best thing about my teacher is the way he smiles at me. (Age 5)

The best thing about my teacher is that she teaches and teaches and teaches her hardest. (Age 9)

The best thing about my teacher is she gives us presents, like books to read. (Age 12)

ABCDEFGHIJKLMNOPQRSTUVWXYZ
abcdefghijklmnopqrstuvwxyz 1234567890

The best thing about my teacher is she loves to be our teacher, and keeps in touch with us as we go through life. (Age 17)

The best thing about my teacher is she listens to us. (Age 7)

The best thing about my teacher is she teaches me how to live in the real world. (Age 11)

6

ABCDEFGHIJKLMNOPQRSTUVWXYZ
abcdefghijklmnopqrstuvwxyz 1234567890

The best thing about my teacher is when I get to work with her at circle time. (Age 5)

The best thing about my teacher is he wants to teach people something and he cares. (Age 18)

The best thing about my teacher is she tells us what to do and doesn't drone on for days. (Age 14)

ABCDEFGHIJKLMNOPQRSTUVWXYZ
abcdefghijklmnopqrstuvwxyz 1234567890

The best thing about my teacher is I like to read
and she lets us read a lot. (Age 8)

The best thing about my teacher is she is always
there for me. (Age 11)

The best thing about my teacher is when she says,
"Meet me at the rectangle rug,"
and she reads me a story. (Age 5)

ABCDEFGHIJKLMNOPQRSTUVWXYZ
abcdefghijklmnopqrstuvwxyz 1234567890

The best thing about my teacher is that he taught me how to play my favorite sport, baseball. (Age 8)

The best thing about my teacher is she is a good person. (Age 6)

The best thing about my teacher is he's real funny sometimes and he likes to teach smaller kids. (Age 9)

ABCDEFGHIJKLMNOPQRSTUVWXYZ
abcdefghijklmnopqrstuvwxyz 1234567890

The best thing about my teacher is she is
very giving. (Age 11)

The best thing about my teacher is that even
though we're in high school, she still reads to us.
(Age 18)

The best thing about my teacher is she lets us have
a teddy bear picnic. (Age 7)

10

ABCDEFGHIJKLMNOPQRSTUVWXYZ
abcdefghijklmnopqrstuvwxyz 1234567890

The best thing about my teacher is she never makes learning boring, she always makes it fun. (Age 9)

The best thing about my teacher is she lets me do hard stuff. (Age 7)

The best thing about my teacher is that he likes to encourage me. (Age 10)

ABCDEFGHIJKLMNOPQRSTUVWXYZ
abcdefghijklmnopqrstuvwxyz 1234567890

The best thing about my teacher is he likes every
kid in the class. (Age 11)

The best thing about my teacher is she lets us go
outside in the rain. (Age 6)

The best thing about my teacher is she laughs at
our jokes and cries when we are sad. (Age 16)

ABCDEFGHIJKLMNOPQRSTUVWXYZ
abcdefghijklmnopqrstuvwxyz 1234567890

The best thing about my teacher is she lets us
wear slippers on muddy days. (Age 7)

The best thing about my teacher is
she gives us candy when she is proud of us
and she smiles really great. (Age 9)

The best thing about my teacher is her tea.
It smells wonderful. I would drink it
if I had a chance. (Age 10)

13

ABCDEFGHIJKLMNOPQRSTUVWXYZ
abcdefghijklmnopqrstuvwxyz 1234567890

The best thing about my teacher is that she puts
up a mind jogger and extra credit book report.
(Age 8)

The best thing about my teacher is
he is fun and fair. (Age 9)

The best thing about my teacher is she has
imagination and is nice. (Age 7)

14

ABCDEFGHIJKLMNOPQRSTUVWXYZ
abcdefghijklmnopqrstuvwxyz 1234567890

The best thing about my teacher is she
teaches us to write on paper. (Age 5)

The best thing about my teacher is when she gets
a fun idea. (Age 10)

The best thing about my teacher is she
understands kids and doesn't talk to us like babies.
(Age 12)

ABCDEFGHIJKLMNOPQRSTUVWXYZ
abcdefghijklmnopqrstuvwxyz 1234567890

The best thing about my teacher
is he is cool. (Age 11)

The best thing about my teacher is
she doesn't yell at me. (Age 7)

The best thing about my teacher is she lets us
bring footballs to school. (Age 8)

16

ABCDEFGHIJKLMNOPQRSTUVWXYZ
abcdefghijklmnopqrstuvwxyz 1234567890

The best thing about my teacher is she likes math and PE, and I like math and PE. (Age 9)

The best thing about my teacher is she is forgiving. (Age 16)

The best thing about my teacher is his creativity! (Age 17)

ABCDEFGHIJKLMNOPQRSTUVWXYZ
abcdefghijklmnopqrstuvwxyz 1234567890

The best thing about my teacher is she always says
I was really good after school. (Age 5)

The best thing about my teacher is she is fun and
she takes the class fun places. (Age 9)

The best thing about my teacher is she always
forgets everything. (Age 6)

18

ABCDEFGHIJKLMNOPQRSTUVWXYZ
abcdefghijklmnopqrstuvwxyz 1234567890

The best thing about my teacher is she's not just a
teacher, she's my friend. (Age 7)

The best thing about my teacher is she always
listens to what I have to say. (Age 13)

The best thing about my teacher is that she sings
to us. (Age 11)

ABCDEFGHIJKLMNOPQRSTUVWXYZ
abcdefghijklmnopqrstuvwxyz 1234567890

The best thing about my teacher is that she's kind and understanding. I know I can always talk to her if I'm troubled. (Age 17)

The best thing about my teacher is he is really fun. (Age 16)

The best thing about my teacher is that she is good to me. (Age 6)

20

ABCDEFGHIJKLMNOPQRSTUVWXYZ
abcdefghijklmnopqrstuvwxyz 1234567890

The best thing about my teacher is her smile. She has a warm heart and a kind face. (Age 10)

The best thing about my teacher is she is nice and understanding, and knows how to teach. (Age 14)

The best thing about my teacher is she lets us be very creative with our work. (Age 9)

21

ABCDEFGHIJKLMNOPQRSTUVWXYZ
abcdefghijklmnopqrstuvwxyz 1234567890

The best thing about my teacher is how much she cares, and how she wants more than anything for us to learn. (Age 14)

The best thing about my teacher is she likes to kid around. (Age 10)

The best thing about my teacher is she understands me. (Age 15)

ABCDEFGHIJKLMNOPQRSTUVWXYZ
abcdefghijklmnopqrstuvwxyz 1234567890

The best thing about my teacher is
she likes me a lot. (Age 7)

The best thing about my teacher is we pick a goal
and she helps us get there. (Age 9)

The best thing about my teacher is she knows how
to comfort me and how to heal what is broken
inside of me. (Age 18)

ABCDEFGHIJKLMNOPQRSTUVWXYZ
abcdefghijklmnopqrstuvwxyz 1234567890

The best thing about my teacher is she teaches me
tons of things that I didn't even know. (Age 8)

The best thing about my teacher is
he has a sense of humor. (Age 11)

The best thing about my teacher is how relaxed
and nice she is in almost all situations. (Age 14)

ABCDEFGHIJKLMNOPQRSTUVWXYZ
abcdefghijklmnopqrstuvwxyz 1234567890

The best thing about my teacher is he gives me a high five. (Age 8)

The best thing about my teacher is she is not mean. (Age 9)

The best thing about my teacher is she can sit down with me and be a person rather than a preacher. She will listen to me. (Age 19)

ABCDEFGHIJKLMNOPQRSTUVWXYZ
abcdefghijklmnopqrstuvwxyz 1234567890

The best thing about my teacher is she listens to us and has a lot of patience. (Age 15)

The best thing about my teacher is when he plays and makes jokes. (Age 11)

The best thing about my teacher is she has a turtle. (Age 6)

ABCDEFGHIJKLMNOPQRSTUVWXYZ
abcdefghijklmnopqrstuvwxyz 1234567890

The best thing about my teacher is she understood when my mom took me out of school on holidays because of our religion. (Age 11)

The best thing about my teacher is she's a happy lady. (Age 5)

The best thing about my teacher is he is a Christian just like me! (Age 9)

ABCDEFGHIJKLMNOPQRSTUVWXYZ
abcdefghijklmnopqrstuvwxyz 1234567890

The best thing about my teacher is she is young and
so she knows how to hang with us. (Age 14)

The best thing about my teacher is that she can
make us shoot a basketball really good. (Age 9)

The best thing about my teacher is that she is
sweet and creative. (Age 11)

ABCDEFGHIJKLMNOPQRSTUVWXYZ
abcdefghijklmnopqrstuvwxyz 1234567890

The best thing about my teacher is her way of understanding and explaining things. (Age 15)

The best thing about my teacher is that she is fun to play with. (Age 8)

The best thing about my teacher is the way she likes me and our class too. (Age 6)

ABCDEFGHIJKLMNOPQRSTUVWXYZ
abcdefghijklmnopqrstuvwxyz 1234567890

The best thing about my teacher is
she gives essays. (Age 7)

The best thing about my teacher is she almost
always can keep a smile on her face. (Age 14)

The best thing about my teacher
is her laugh. (Age 8)

My Teacher . . .

ABCDEFGHIJKLMNOPQRSTUVWXYZ
abcdefghijklmnopqrstuvwxyz 1234567890

My teacher shows me the world! (Age 11)

My teacher is the bestest teacher in the world.
(Age 5)

My teacher wants only the best for her students.
(Age 17)

My teacher always crosses her legs
when she sits down. (Age 6)

ABCDEFGHIJKLMNOPQRSTUVWXYZ
abcdefghijklmnopqrstuvwxyz 1234567890

My teacher is kind to me. (Age 5)

My teacher is a boy. (Age 10)

My teacher is like a bee coming around to help all
the kids even if they are not in her class. (Age 9)

My teacher likes my attitude. (Age 7)

ABCDEFGHIJKLMNOPQRSTUVWXYZ
abcdefghijklmnopqrstuvwxyz 1234567890

My teacher lets us play on the big kids' playground sometimes. (Age 5)

My teacher can read well. (Age 8)

My teacher is always excited to teach us new things. (Age 17)

My teacher gets TWO milks with his lunch and a LOT of food. (Age 5)

ABCDEFGHIJKLMNOPQRSTUVWXYZ
abcdefghijklmnopqrstuvwxyz 1234567890

My teacher makes funny jokes and has a pet rat.
(Age 11)

My teacher is kind, caring, and very attentive to
her students and their problems. (Age 17)

My teacher is nice like sugar and spice. (Age 9)

My teacher plays music for us on the piano. (Age 12)

ABCDEFGHIJKLMNOPQRSTUVWXYZ
abcdefghijklmnopqrstuvwxyz 1234567890

My teacher buys groceries. I saw him at the store. I guess he eats food too. (Age 5)

My teacher is a friend who teaches me valuable lessons about life. (Age 18)

My teacher is really nice and she looks like a lady on a magazine. (Age 6)

ABCDEFGHIJKLMNOPQRSTUVWXYZ
abcdefghijklmnopqrstuvwxyz 1234567890

My teacher reads funny and silly stories. (Age 8)

My teacher colors good. (Age 9)

My teacher lets us play with lots of toys. (Age 6)

My teacher responds to questions and helps me
when I need help with an assignment. (Age 10)

My teacher has a lot of kids in her class. (Age 5)

ABCDEFGHIJKLMNOPQRSTUVWXYZ
abcdefghijklmnopqrstuvwxyz 1234567890

My teacher is a wonderful person
most of the time. (Age 19)

My teacher, I hug every day. (Age 5)

My teacher is smart and nice. I hope she teaches
us to be smart and nice too. (Age 9)

My teacher is nice because she lets me do math.
(Age 8)

ABCDEFGHIJKLMNOPQRSTUVWXYZ
abcdefghijklmnopqrstuvwxyz 1234567890

My teacher is nice and I like the snacks. (Age 5)

My teacher is sooo nice. She lets us do whatever
we want, but not really. (Age 6)

My teacher is very nice and polite. (Age 7)

My teacher is nice because she gives
diligent worker points for good things
and grades. (Age 10)

ABCDEFGHIJKLMNOPQRSTUVWXYZ
abcdefghijklmnopqrstuvwxyz 1234567890

My teacher probably doesn't drink beer. (Age 5)

My teacher is a very creative person and has great work ideas that help us to get the most out of our learning. (Age 16)

My teacher is a good soccer player. (Age 9)

My teacher is always well organized. (Age 14)

ABCDEFGHIJKLMNOPQRSTUVWXYZ
abcdefghijklmnopqrstuvwxyz 1234567890

My teacher always lets us do fun stuff like play a
game called heads up, five up. (Age 7)

My teacher is not beautiful. He is a man. (Age 5)

My teacher gives me strength to do things
I never thought I could do. She gives me
strength from the inside. (Age 18)

ABCDEFGHIJKLMNOPQRSTUVWXYZ
abcdefghijklmnopqrstuvwxyz 1234567890

My teacher takes care of all the kids. (Age 5)

My teacher is very, very funny
and I know a lot about her. (Age 8)

My teacher is funny, smart, and very cool. (Age 9)

My teacher is very strict, but is funny. (Age 10)

ABCDEFGHIJKLMNOPQRSTUVWXYZ
abcdefghijklmnopqrstuvwxyz 1234567890

My teacher is very funny and teaches good math.
(Age 11)

My teacher is funny and sings to us. (Age 12)

My teacher knows the rules a lot better than us.
He's older. (Age 5)

ABCDEFGHIJKLMNOPQRSTUVWXYZ
abcdefghijklmnopqrstuvwxyz 1234567890

My teacher is great because she helps me
use my imagination. (Age 6)

My teacher has a lot of patience. (Age 15)

My teacher told us how to make gingerbread men.
(Age 7)

ABCDEFGHIJKLMNOPQRSTUVWXYZ
abcdefghijklmnopqrstuvwxyz 1234567890

My teacher smiles too much.
He LOVES smiling. (Age 5)

My teacher has a great love for what she does and
has a place in every student's heart. (Age 17)

My teacher is smart and makes us smarter. (Age 7)

My teacher is also my buddy. (Age 14)

ABCDEFGHIJKLMNOPQRSTUVWXYZ
abcdefghijklmnopqrstuvwxyz 1234567890

My teacher likes my apple pencil I gave her. (Age 5)

My teacher likes me so much! (Age 5)

My teacher is a really cool, down-to-earth person.
(Age 12)

My teacher is a good drawer, a good respect
teacher, and he is a good learner. (Age 8)

ABCDEFGHIJKLMNOPQRSTUVWXYZ
abcdefghijklmnopqrstuvwxyz 1234567890

My teacher has recess duty. (Age 6)

My teacher plays with me. (Age 7)

My teacher gives us really hard work. (Age 6)

My teacher always understands. (Age 9)

My teacher is jolly and can always
give a hand. (Age 10)

ABCDEFGHIJKLMNOPQRSTUVWXYZ
abcdefghijklmnopqrstuvwxyz 1234567890

My teacher points with her pinkie
when she shows us maps. (Age 7)

My teacher never sends kids to the office. (Age 5)

My teacher puts me in different moods.
She makes me nervous, relaxed, stressed out,
and under control. (Age 16)

ABCDEFGHIJKLMNOPQRSTUVWXYZ
abcdefghijklmnopqrstuvwxyz 1234567890

My teacher wears a fancy suit sometimes. (Age 5)

My teacher is beautiful and her
favorite color is green. (Age 7)

My teacher works at the school. (Age 7)

My teacher is my personal adviser, hero, and friend.
(Age 12)

ABCDEFGHIJKLMNOPQRSTUVWXYZ
abcdefghijklmnopqrstuvwxyz 1234567890

My teacher is nice because he gives me
extra homework. (Age 8)

My teacher shows me the skills I need in life.
(Age 10)

My teacher talks nice to me. (Age 5)

My teacher is the key to success. (Age 11)

50

ABCDEFGHIJKLMNOPQRSTUVWXYZ
abcdefghijklmnopqrstuvwxyz 1234567890

My teacher is unique just like all her students.
(Age 15)

My teacher taught me how to play basketball.
(Age 9)

My teacher teaches me about amphibians. (Age 8)

My teacher takes his Bible with him to church.
(Age 5)

ABCDEFGHIJKLMNOPQRSTUVWXYZ
abcdefghijklmnopqrstuvwxyz 1234567890

My teacher is a very positive influence
and I highly respect her, for she is preparing
my path to college. (Age 17)

My teacher, I love her. (Age 5)

I Like It When My Teacher . . .

ABCDEFGHIJKLMNOPQRSTUVWXYZ
abcdefghijklmnopqrstuvwxyz 1234567890

I like it when my teacher says,
"Time to clean up." (Age 5)

I like it when my teacher is funny with me
and my friends. (Age 11)

I like it when my teacher gives me a bear hug
before the weekend. (Age 12)

54

ABCDEFGHIJKLMNOPQRSTUVWXYZ
abcdefghijklmnopqrstuvwxyz 1234567890

I like it when my teacher buys new toys. (Age 5)

I like it when my teacher teaches me about great
American novels and stories by going over them with
me until I understand. (Age 17)

I like it when my teacher gives us work. (Age 7)

ABCDEFGHIJKLMNOPQRSTUVWXYZ
abcdefghijklmnopqrstuvwxyz 1234567890

I like it when my teacher doesn't give us homework.
(Age 11)

I like it when my teacher lets us sit on our desks.
(Age 8)

I like it that my teacher took us on a trip and we
saw *The Sound of Music.* (Age 12)

56

ABCDEFGHIJKLMNOPQRSTUVWXYZ
abcdefghijklmnopqrstuvwxyz 1234567890

I like it when my teacher has a heart. (Age 6)

I like it when my teacher gets so flustered that
she has to sit down and remember what she was
going to do. (Age 17)

I like it when my teacher teaches us
new games in PE. (Age 9)

ABCDEFGHIJKLMNOPQRSTUVWXYZ
abcdefghijklmnopqrstuvwxyz 1234567890

I like it when my teacher asks me to
"freeze." (Age 5)

I like it when my teacher plays around and isn't
serious. (Age 11)

I like it when my teacher takes her doggy
to school. (Age 11)

ABCDEFGHIJKLMNOPQRSTUVWXYZ
abcdefghijklmnopqrstuvwxyz 1234567890

I like it when my teacher explains in a fashion that
is permanently embedded in my mind,
not to be forgotten. (Age 18)

I like it when my teacher loves me. (Age 7)

I like it when my teacher cooks with us. (Age 5)

ABCDEFGHIJKLMNOPQRSTUVWXYZ
abcdefghijklmnopqrstuvwxyz 1234567890

I like it when my teacher has class discussions
where everyone has a chance to speak their minds.
(Age 14)

I like it when my teacher says I am paying
attention. (Age 8)

I like it when my teacher can relate to
what I am saying. (Age 17)

ABCDEFGHIJKLMNOPQRSTUVWXYZ
abcdefghijklmnopqrstuvwxyz 1234567890

I like it when my teacher teaches math because she makes it fun, and I learn a lot about numbers and coins. (Age 6)

I like it when my teacher reads to us in funny voices. (Age 9)

I like it when my teacher talks to us about things other than the subject. (Age 12)

ABCDEFGHIJKLMNOPQRSTUVWXYZ
abcdefghijklmnopqrstuvwxyz 1234567890

I like it when my teacher plays with us at recess.
(Age 8)

I like it when my teacher doesn't interrupt me.
(Age 7)

I like it when my teacher gives us pizza when we
have perfect attendance. (Age 11)

ABCDEFGHIJKLMNOPQRSTUVWXYZ
abcdefghijklmnopqrstuvwxyz 1234567890

I like it when my teacher lets us goof off in class—within reason, of course! (Age 14)

I like it when my teacher teaches me how to play. (Age 5)

I like it when my teacher does something nice for me and I appreciate it. (Age 8)

63

ABCDEFGHIJKLMNOPQRSTUVWXYZ
abcdefghijklmnopqrstuvwxyz 1234567890

I like it when my teacher does art with us. (Age 9)

I like it when my teacher is in a good, humorous
mood. It puts us all in a good mood. (Age 13)

I like it when my teacher is on yard duty
because that means we get to go
in the sandbox. (Age 5)

ABCDEFGHIJKLMNOPQRSTUVWXYZ
abcdefghijklmnopqrstuvwxyz 1234567890

I like it when my teacher displays my work. (Age 12)

I like it when my teacher raffles things off to the class. Because there's a good chance I will win. (Age 9)

I like it when my teacher lets us watch movies in class on rainy days. (Age 9)

ABCDEFGHIJKLMNOPQRSTUVWXYZ
abcdefghijklmnopqrstuvwxyz 1234567890

I like it when my teacher helps me jump rope.
(Age 6)

I like it when my teacher overreacts about things.
She always gets really excited if we do
something she likes. (Age 14)

I like it when my teacher does parties for us.
(Age 9)

66

A B C D E F G H I J K L M N O P Q R S T U V W X Y Z
abcdefghijklmnopqrstuvwxyz 1234567890

I like it when my teacher gives out popcorn
tickets for doing good work so we can get prizes.
(Age 11)

I like it when my teacher helps me peel my orange.
(Age 5)

I like it when my teacher puts in marbles
when I'm good. (Age 7)

ABCDEFGHIJKLMNOPQRSTUVWXYZ
abcdefghijklmnopqrstuvwxyz 1234567890

I like it when my teacher is nice to me. (Age 6)

I like it when my teacher makes us do hard labor.
(Age 8)

I like it when my teacher is happy with us or when
she gets good news about our class. (Age 9)

I like it when my teacher takes us to the pizza
place for lunch. (Age 10)

ABCDEFGHIJKLMNOPQRSTUVWXYZ
abcdefghijklmnopqrstuvwxyz 1234567890

I like it when my teacher reads aloud because
it makes me have a picture in my head of
what she's reading. (Age 9)

I like it when my teacher laughs. (Age 7)

I like it when my teacher makes jokes. (Age 14)

ABCDEFGHIJKLMNOPQRSTUVWXYZ
abcdefghijklmnopqrstuvwxyz 1234567890

I like it when my teacher pulls out the lipstick.
(Age 12)
Teacher's explanation: The "lipstick" is a glue stick.
When someone is talking excessively,
I offer them my special lipstick.

I like it when my teacher does fun things
for PE like dancing. (Age 9)

I like it when my teacher helps us with our
homework when it is hard. (Age 12)

I like it when my teacher smiles at me. (Age 6)

I like it when my teacher is happy. (Age 8)

I like it when my teacher gives me hugs. (Age 9)

ABCDEFGHIJKLMNOPQRSTUVWXYZ
abcdefghijklmnopqrstuvwxyz 1234567890

I like it when my teacher talks to me
outside at recess. (Age 5)

I like it when my teacher tells stories
about his life. (Age 9)

I like it when my teacher does something new
almost every day. (Age 10)

ABCDEFGHIJKLMNOPQRSTUVWXYZ
abcdefghijklmnopqrstuvwxyz 1234567890

I like it when my teacher reads. He has a perfect voice for the characters. (Age 9)

I like it when my teacher acts like us. (Age 14)

I like it when my teacher talks about something that you bring up, and he just goes off and makes you understand it. (Age 19)

ABCDEFGHIJKLMNOPQRSTUVWXYZ
abcdefghijklmnopqrstuvwxyz 1234567890

I like it when my teacher holds my hand when we
are in line. (Age 6)

I like it when my teacher rides her bike. (Age 7)

I like it when my teacher sends the cute little
postcards to remind us, her students, that she
loves us and will always be there for us. (Age 17)

ABCDEFGHIJKLMNOPQRSTUVWXYZ
abcdefghijklmnopqrstuvwxyz 1234567890

I like it when my teacher leaves the classroom and we can talk among ourselves and laugh. (Age 14)

I like it when my teacher reads our literature books to us because she is a good, dramatic reader. (Age 16)

I like it when my teacher always takes an interest in my life and its direction. (Age 18)

75

ABCDEFGHIJKLMNOPQRSTUVWXYZ
abcdefghijklmnopqrstuvwxyz 1234567890

I like it when my teacher plays the piano in the gym.
(Age 8)

I like it when my teacher compliments me
for some things I do. (Age 13)

I like it when my teacher makes funny faces.
(Age 8)

ABCDEFGHIJKLMNOPQRSTUVWXYZ
abcdefghijklmnopqrstuvwxyz 1234567890

I like it when my teacher smiles and laughs, so that
we can laugh together as a class. (Age 18)

I like it when my teacher tells stories about the
places he has been and the things he has done.
(Age 17)

77

ABCDEFGHIJKLMNOPQRSTUVWXYZ
abcdefghijklmnopqrstuvwxyz 1234567890

I like it when my teacher teaches with objects so the lessons are funner and make more sense.
(Age 11)

I like it when my teacher has faith in me that I can get the job done. (Age 16)

I like it when my teacher is fair to all the students. (Age 14)

ABCDEFGHIJKLMNOPQRSTUVWXYZ
abcdefghijklmnopqrstuvwxyz 1234567890

I like it when my teacher lets us play with toys.
(Age 5)

I like it when my teacher takes the time to help me
out when I need her to. (Age 17)

I like it when my teacher writes me letters and
tells me I did a good job. (Age 6)

ABCDEFGHIJKLMNOPQRSTUVWXYZ
abcdefghijklmnopqrstuvwxyz 1234567890

I like it when my teacher picks me for student of the day. (Age 10)

I like it when my teacher gives us a study period! (Age 17)

I like it when my teacher says it's time for recess. (Age 8)

ABCDEFGHIJKLMNOPQRSTUVWXYZ
abcdefghijklmnopqrstuvwxyz 1234567890

I like it when my teacher helps those who don't understand and does it without yelling. (Age 19)

I like it when my teacher gives me a "gallant" when I do a good thing. (Age 5)

I like it when my teacher gives us a stretch break. (Age 10)

ABCDEFGHIJKLMNOPQRSTUVWXYZ
abcdefghijklmnopqrstuvwxyz 1234567890

I like it when my teacher plays games with me.
(Age 8)

I like it when my teacher encourages me
to do my best. (Age 7)

I like it when my teacher reads me Jesus stories
so I can learn about Jesus. (Age 8)

Thank You, Teacher . . .

ABCDEFGHIJKLMNOPQRSTUVWXYZ
abcdefghijklmnopqrstuvwxyz 1234567890

Thank you, teacher, for seeing me. (Age 5)

Thank you, teacher, for reading books to me. I liked the one about the dressed-up giant. (Age 5)

Thank you, teacher, for the present. (Age 5)

Thank you, teacher, for letting me play. (Age 5)

Thank you, teacher, for my "at-home" reading books. (Age 5)

84

ABCDEFGHIJKLMNOPQRSTUVWXYZ
abcdefghijklmnopqrstuvwxyz 1234567890

Thank you, teacher, for giving me a Band-Aid! (Age 5)

Thank you, teacher, for giving me an award for helping out in class. (Age 5)

Thank you, teacher, for holding my backpack. (Age 5)

Thank you, teacher, for letting us make snowmen. (Age 5)

ABCDEFGHIJKLMNOPQRSTUVWXYZ
abcdefghijklmnopqrstuvwxyz 1234567890

Thank you, teacher, for letting me go home. (Age 5)

Thank you, teacher, for teaching me how to read.
(Age 6)

Thank you, teacher, for helping me write. (Age 6)

Thank you, teacher, for the happy faces. (Age 6)

Thank you, teacher, for loving me. (Age 6)

ABCDEFGHIJKLMNOPQRSTUVWXYZ
abcdefghijklmnopqrstuvwxyz 1234567890

Thank you, teacher, for showing us all the things that we could do. (Age 6)

Thank you, teacher, for recess. (Age 6)

Thank you, teacher, for homework. (Age 6)

Thank you, teacher, for letting us have free choice. (Age 6)

ABCDEFGHIJKLMNOPQRSTUVWXYZ
abcdefghijklmnopqrstuvwxyz 1234567890

Thank you, teacher, for reading so many books.
(Age 6)

Thank you, teacher, for making the word wall.
(Age 6)

Thank you, teacher, for the nice classroom
with all the books and toys. (Age 6)

Thank you, teacher, for making school fun. (Age 6)

88

ABCDEFGHIJKLMNOPQRSTUVWXYZ
abcdefghijklmnopqrstuvwxyz 1234567890

Thank you, teacher, for teaching me
take-away in math. (Age 7)

Thank you, teacher, for giving all of us cookies.
(Age 7)

Thank you, teacher, for showing us amphibians. (Age 7)

Thank you, teacher, for telling us
about ecosystems. (Age 7)

89

ABCDEFGHIJKLMNOPQRSTUVWXYZ
abcdefghijklmnopqrstuvwxyz 1234567890

Thank you, teacher, for how we did our calendars.
(Age 7)

Thank you, teacher, for the book and tin of candy
you gave me for being a good girl. (Age 7)

Thank you, teacher, for teaching us how to write
long words like Mississippi. (Age 7)

ABCDEFGHIJKLMNOPQRSTUVWXYZ
abcdefghijklmnopqrstuvwxyz 1234567890

Thank you, teacher, for making up the lunch bunch.
(Age 7)

Thank you, teacher, for taking us on field trips.
(Age 8)

Thank you, teacher, for giving me good work and
giving me treats. (Age 8)

91

ABCDEFGHIJKLMNOPQRSTUVWXYZ
abcdefghijklmnopqrstuvwxyz 1234567890

Thank you, teacher, for the letter you sent me.
(Age 8)

Thank you, teacher, for letting us have extra
recess. (Age 8)

Thank you, teacher, for all the parties and all the
fun things you do for us. (Age 8)

Thank you, teacher, for liking me a lot. (Age 8)

ABCDEFGHIJKLMNOPQRSTUVWXYZ
abcdefghijklmnopqrstuvwxyz 1234567890

Thank you, teacher, for teaching me
to pitch and hit. (Age 8)

Thank you, teacher, for helping me with my work and
keeping me safe at school. (Age 8)

Thank you, teacher, for letting me have
colored pencils. (Age 8)

93

ABCDEFGHIJKLMNOPQRSTUVWXYZ
abcdefghijklmnopqrstuvwxyz 1234567890

Thank you, teacher, for helping me correct mistakes and to make them become the right punctuation. (Age 8)

Thank you, teacher, for teaching us to be good sports. (Age 9)

Thank you, teacher, for being a nice teacher and appreciating everyone's different talents. (Age 9)

ABCDEFGHIJKLMNOPQRSTUVWXYZ
abcdefghijklmnopqrstuvwxyz 1234567890

Thank you, teacher, for cupcakes. (Age 9)

Thank you, teacher, for always caring and being responsible and loving. (Age 9)

Thank you, teacher, for always being there for me. (Age 9)

Thank you, teacher, for making it fun to learn. (Age 9)

ABCDEFGHIJKLMNOPQRSTUVWXYZ
abcdefghijklmnopqrstuvwxyz 1234567890

Thank you, teacher, for making us smart, patient,
and quiet in class. (Age 9)

Thank you, teacher, for making me
see things better. (Age 9)

Thank you, teacher, for teaching me all the
things you know. (Age 9)

ABCDEFGHIJKLMNOPQRSTUVWXYZ
abcdefghijklmnopqrstuvwxyz 1234567890

Thank you, teacher, for making this year
the funnest. (Age 9)

Thank you, teacher, for teaching me how to do
times tables. (Age 10)

Thank you, teacher, for making me improve
in school studies. (Age 10)

ABCDEFGHIJKLMNOPQRSTUVWXYZ
abcdefghijklmnopqrstuvwxyz 1234567890

Thank you, teacher, for being patient and not
yelling all the time. (Age 10)

Thank you, teacher, for being a real fun teacher.
(Age 10)

Thank you, teacher, for all the things
you've done for us. (Age 10)

ABCDEFGHIJKLMNOPQRSTUVWXYZ
abcdefghijklmnopqrstuvwxyz 1234567890

Thank you, teacher, for being so nice to all of us kids. (Age 10)

Thank you, teacher, for helping me with stuff I get stuck on. (Age 11)

Thank you, teacher, for being the best teacher I know. If you were to fall down a well the whole world would feel sorrow. (Age 11)

ABCDEFGHIJKLMNOPQRSTUVWXYZ
abcdefghijklmnopqrstuvwxyz 1234567890

Thank you, teacher, for the gift of your smile. (Age 11)

Thank you, teacher, for being a good teacher and giving me great memories about the past. (Age 11)

Thank you, teacher, for being funny and doing the voices at read-aloud. (Age 11)

Thank you, teacher, for caring about us through thick and thin. (Age 11)

100

ABCDEFGHIJKLMNOPQRSTUVWXYZ
abcdefghijklmnopqrstuvwxyz 1234567890

Thank you, teacher, for telling me never to eat a jalapeno burger. My friend did once and she couldn't talk for ten minutes. (Age 11)

Thank you, teacher, for having us make globes. (Age 11)

Thank you, teacher, for committing so much of your time to help me succeed. (Age 11)

ABCDEFGHIJKLMNOPQRSTUVWXYZ
abcdefghijklmnopqrstuvwxyz 1234567890

Thank you, teacher, for helping us learn and having patience with us when we didn't understand.
(Age 11)

Thank you, teacher, for believing in me. (Age 11)

Thank you, teacher, for being very nice to me and not making me feel bad. (Age 11)

ABCDEFGHIJKLMNOPQRSTUVWXYZ
abcdefghijklmnopqrstuvwxyz 1234567890

Thank you, teacher, for treating me like a human, not like a baby or a monster. (Age 12)

Thank you, teacher, for teaching me many great things in this world. (Age 12)

Thank you, teacher, for everything you have done for me. You were always there for me. (Age 12)

ABCDEFGHIJKLMNOPQRSTUVWXYZ
abcdefghijklmnopqrstuvwxyz 1234567890

Thank you, teacher, for encouraging us to
ask questions. (Age 12)

Thank you, teacher, for giving me the best
education I could get. (Age 12)

Thank you, teacher, for understanding me. You have
taught me how to understand myself and others.
(Age 13)

ABCDEFGHIJKLMNOPQRSTUVWXYZ
abcdefghijklmnopqrstuvwxyz 1234567890

Thank you, teacher, for always helping me, even when I was struggling. (Age 13)

Thank you, teacher, for making my life at school exciting and full of "color." (Age 13)

Thank you, teacher, for having a great attitude and an open mind. (Age 13)

ABCDEFGHIJKLMNOPQRSTUVWXYZ
abcdefghijklmnopqrstuvwxyz 1234567890

Thank you, teacher, for giving me the courage to speak in public. (Age 13)

Thank you, teacher, for letting me learn all the things you have taught me so I can follow my dreams. (Age 13)

Thank you, teacher, for being concerned about everyone's grades. (Age 14)

ABCDEFGHIJKLMNOPQRSTUVWXYZ
abcdefghijklmnopqrstuvwxyz 1234567890

Thank you, teacher, for not making jokes about me!
(Age 14)

Thank you, teacher, for dealing with all the kids and
helping the good ones and bad ones. (Age 14)

Thank you, teacher, for not being a pain
about homework. (Age 14)

ABCDEFGHIJKLMNOPQRSTUVWXYZ
abcdefghijklmnopqrstuvwxyz 1234567890

Thank you, teacher, for being so nice
and understanding. (Age 14)

Thank you, teacher, for preparing me for the
rest of my life and future. (Age 14)

Thank you, teacher, for making art class
exciting and different. (Age 15)

ABCDEFGHIJKLMNOPQRSTUVWXYZ
abcdefghijklmnopqrstuvwxyz 1234567890

Thank you, teacher, for getting me interested
in short stories. (Age 15)

Thank you, teacher, for having tolerance and
listening when we have something to say. (Age 15)

Thank you, teacher, for helping me through the year.
(Age 15)

ABCDEFGHIJKLMNOPQRSTUVWXYZ
abcdefghijklmnopqrstuvwxyz 1234567890

Thank you, teacher, for reading to us after lunch.
That is fun. (Age 15)

Thank you, teacher, for teaching, which is the
greatest gift. (Age 15)

Thank you, teacher, for being cool. (Age 15)

ABCDEFGHIJKLMNOPQRSTUVWXYZ
abcdefghijklmnopqrstuvwxyz 1234567890

Thank you, teacher, for giving me the benefit of the doubt. (Age 16)

Thank you, teacher, for helping me feel confident about myself and my ability to think to the best of my ability. (Age 16)

Thank you, teacher, for your kind words of encouragement. (Age 16)

ABCDEFGHIJKLMNOPQRSTUVWXYZ
abcdefghijklmnopqrstuvwxyz 1234567890

Thank you, teacher, for being so caring and
concerned about my well-being,
not just my school work. (Age 16)

Thank you, teacher, for being relaxed and not
uptight with our class. (Age 16)

Thank you, teacher, for helping me with everything.
(Age 16)

ABCDEFGHIJKLMNOPQRSTUVWXYZ
abcdefghijklmnopqrstuvwxyz 1234567890

Thank you, teacher, for caring enough about me to not accept anything but my best. (Age 17)

Thank you, teacher, for being a friend, interesting and fun. (Age 17)

ABCDEFGHIJKLMNOPQRSTUVWXYZ
abcdefghijklmnopqrstuvwxyz 1234567890

Thank you, teacher, for showing me that to be yourself is to be an achiever in life. (Age 17)

Thank you, teacher, for instilling the power and knowledge to accomplish anything. (Age 17)

Thank you, teacher, for always making me stay on task and get my work done. (Age 17)

ABCDEFGHIJKLMNOPQRSTUVWXYZ
abcdefghijklmnopqrstuvwxyz 1234567890

Thank you, teacher, for caring enough to make sure
I succeeded. (Age 17)

Thank you, teacher, for helping me show
all my abilities. (Age 17)

Thank you, teacher, for always making me feel as
special as if I were your only student
in the whole world. (Age 17)

ABCDEFGHIJKLMNOPQRSTUVWXYZ
abcdefghijklmnopqrstuvwxyz 1234567890

Thank you, teacher, for taking the time to help me better understand life and myself. (Age 18)

Thank you, teacher, for helping me stand and never letting me fall. You are my kindred spirit. (Age 18)

Thank you, teacher, for giving me chances to get my act together. (Age 18)

ABCDEFGHIJKLMNOPQRSTUVWXYZ
abcdefghijklmnopqrstuvwxyz 1234567890

Thank you, teacher, for going far beyond your teaching duties and being there as a friend.
(Age 18)

Thank you, teacher, for always being there and telling me that I do a good job. It gives me confidence. (Age 19)